# The Dark Side

Poems by

Natalie Tiik

For two people who understand more than they
know about mental health.


For the two people that got me through it.


Hyde
&
Spitty.

Crazy things happen all over the world.

Uno Tiik

**Table of Contents:**

Illness

Withdrawal

Time

Self-harm

Doormat

Circles

Dad: The best thing

Reality

Madgalene

Idolised couple

Uno

The future

# Grief

One minute you are so far from understanding
it

You are like an ostrich

Its head looking up into a clear blue
cloudless sky without a care in the world.

Suddenly, the moment comes

The head falls down and races underground

The soil suffocates it

It's dark, it is lonely and cold

Not the temperature but it makes your hair
stand on its end

Straight like a ruler

So dominant and proud to be controlling you

It is a feeling of emptiness

An incredible, heavy emptiness that seems to
weigh you down

An egg timer that seems not to end
It never ends

Sometimes the sand gets stuck in the funnel

But it starts again and again

For both the foreseeable and unforeseeable
future

It will always resurface.

Unlike the forever-suffocated ostrich

You know it has always been there and always
will be

You wish it were the person instead.

## Anxiety

Anxiety is like a friendship.

Friendships can be infrequent and often
unsuspected.
They do not appear incriminating in any way.
A friend can enter your life at any time, for
no given reason.

My friend Anxiety did this.

After years of being silent, a true friend can
re-enter your life;
Sometimes when least expected and even
uninvited.
The strongest of friendships can do this.

My friend Anxiety taught me this.

I learnt that it is a feeling that fades but
never completely goes away.

It stays submerged at the bottom of a distant
tomb within you.

It is there for that long that sometimes, and
only sometimes, you can forget it is there at
all.
Like a figment of your imagination.

*This is wrong.*

Anxiety is still your friend.
It's just been busy for a while.
It's been there, watching over you.
Waiting,

Until...

Right there again,
like the time it has been away isn't
significant at all.
Just as good a friend as before
Maybe even a stronger friendship than before.
Powerful.
A focused, feisty, fierce, frightening
friendship and which is now visible for all to
see.

Friendships can sometimes suffocate you.
Those excellent, extrovert friends.
Anxiety is this type of friend.

The friend that is so full on and fanatic you
would like to punch it.
With every bit of energy you have,
From deep down within your tomb.

You think about challenging the friend for a
long time.
You have to challenge them.
The friendship needs to end.

What use is a friendship if it is unhealthy?

You haven't the energy to maintain the
friendship anymore.
You haven't got the time.

I must challenge
I must fight
Throw my punch and push the friendship away.

I will be strong.
I will not let the friendship reunite.
Tomorrow, we won't be friends.

I don't need you anymore, Anxiety;
I feel my closest friend is surplus to
requirements.

Can I really let this friendship end?
A constant battle in my mind.
It knows all my secrets, flaws and
insecurities

*Anxiety controls me.*
It is a courageous, controlling friend.

If you don't do what Anxiety wants, it gets
angry.
It is within me and so will make me angry.
Anger can destroy true friendships.

Anxiety taught me this too.

It is a poisonous friendship and I cannot
trust it.
What is a friendship without trust?
It's time to punch…

Again.

I am terrified when tomorrow arrives that my
friend is still there.
It took all my energy to punch.

I'm not sure that I can I punch again?

I try and fail repeatedly.
I feel failure, and my confidence is lowering
by the minute.
Self-esteem goes down a spiral slide.
It's a waterslide,
going too fast.

It hurts and pains like a burn on the surface
of my skin.

I soon learnt that if you punch, the only
person that gets hurt is yourself.
I know this.

Anxiety taught me this.

Sometimes I may succeed.
Anxiety may go away.

But like a true friend, Anxiety welcomes you
back into its life, with no explanation
required.

I feel I failed as an individual.
I was not strong enough on my own.
I needed my friend back.

The friendship suffocates me from the inside
out,

1. Starting in my stomach.

2. Moving into the chest, and then the most
   unbearable suffocation of all:

3. My thoughts. My cognitive functioning. My
   ability to function daily as a 'normal'
   person.


The suffocation has now surrounded you and
then is back to full force.

It is within me.
It is a part of me.

*Suffocation of the stomach:*

It's a knot within the stomach.
A fisherman's knot.
What use is a feeling if not powerful?
If a job's worth doing, it should be done
right,
Right?

It's the feeling of butterflies fluttering but
just doesn't look as pretty.

They are trapped inside an empty fishbowl,
The tomb within me.

It's the feeling of moths quivering against
the edges.

It's a sparrow frantically flapping to get out
of the bowl,

Not having the ability to stop and think that
there is actually is an escape route.

It just needs to calm down,
control its breathing and focus;

Think rationally.

How can it rationalise its thoughts when one
of Anxiety's strongest characteristics is
irrationality?

It isn't a pleasant image.
It's an uneasy image.

If only the sparrow could look as handsome as
a male robin's beautiful chest.

Your stomach is now a washing machine on a
spin cycle,

matting the insides together.

*Suffocation of the chest:*

It's the experience of falling when asleep and
instantly jolting upright with the spilt-
second of panic.

I'm falling, it wasn't a dream.

I am awake and not alone.

Anxiety holds my hand;

the difference being that it is so much longer
than a spilt second.

A prolonged panic.

It feels like the panic will never be
overcome.

Like taking a long inhale from a cigarette and
not being able to blow out the smoke.

Quickly drowning the airwaves with a grey
cloud of smoke.

Panic riddling your body's organs at an
uncontrollable speed.

The panic of trying to get out of the dark.

The fright as the adrenaline soars through the
body and prepares the nervous system for the
terrifying threat,

Which is now actually only that figment of my imagination.

It's pins and needles in your fingers but actually in the entirety of your chest.

That sting that I experience when breathing hard when running in the cold.

Suffocation of the heart being squeezed by a firm handgrip.

Suffocation of this type is not what you experience in a healthy friendship.

The fisherman then ties his knot back around my chest…

Tightly hugging around my ribs,
the feeling as if you were constantly touching the sore bruises that surround my body.

*The suffocation of my cognitive functioning and my ability to function daily as a 'normal' person:*

Your entirety is now suffocated.
Your personality fighting to get through.
Throwing punches.

It's about making new friends.

Real friends.

Friends support you through Anxiety.

Keep your friends close;
Find an enemy and keep them closer.

Anxiety is now, and I feel will forever be, my enemy.

It's losing 2lbs in a day through the constant jittering of your feet.

It's the irritating fiddling of hands.

The dancing of your fingertips,

the lack of ability to sit still.

It's the looks you receive from people who think you're being impatient;

Rude.

The analysing of conversations and messages,

unreliable irrational interpretations.

The infuriating tone of my voice when someone has interrupted me.

When I'm talking to myself in my own head,

this talking is either rational or irrational;

Mainly irrational.

I use the energy of the adrenaline to fight the irrationalities. I just can't see the difference yet.

It's not being able to listen to conversations.

Cognitions constantly analysing previous ones.

Constantly wondering what the 'real' friend is
thinking –

Why did they say that?

I miss so much of the real world.

I am constantly living in a fantasy with my
imaginary friend,

Anxiety.

It's the swollen-tongue sensation.
Blowing up a waterbomb balloon to its maximum
capacity.

Until it cannot swell any more.

I don't want to think about it.
If I do, it might burst.

I might choke on the water that allowed it to
swell.

It's the grinding of teeth when I'm asleep

The clenching of the jaw

It's so usual, I barely recognise it
until the jaw aches and the teeth grind away

It's the patterns of sleep.

I share my sleep with my friend.

I give too little or too much.

If I don't get enough, my friend is the only
thing that gets me through the day;

Either way, it's a tiring battle.

It's my own anxieties – whether I have I taken my meds…

Have I remembered to take one?

What if I take another and then I have taken too much?

I hope I don't get anxious.

Its self-criticism at its highest.

I must be hated.

I must be wrong.

It's not having a true cure,

A terminal illness without a given time.
It may hinder, it may not.

It may go away but I'm anxious as I'm unsure if my friend will return.

It's the dark black spots that cloud your eyesight when you have almost given in.

You have no control.

You can see nothing but spots.

The most important thing my friend taught me is direction.

I can lose direction in life

I'm at a crossroads but all I can see is some spots.

There is frightening darkness.

I don't know which way to go,

I can only pace.

Pace until I'm too tired,

The only direction I want to go…is away from that friend.

I am an autumn leaf.

Colour gone from my once-youthful skin.

I hang in the balance,
swaying in the wind,
waiting to fall,

To have the moment of prolonged panic, without the waking up and it going away.

I'm waiting for the fall to steer my direction.

There is no direction in life…

Until death.

# Life

Life can take a variety of routes,
The route is mostly unclear.
Sometimes it's a downward slope,
Almost pleasurable.
Mostly bearable.
Other times, it's a steady-paced walk on flat
ground.

It's existence. Simple, mundane.
Occasionally or even regularly it tends to be
uphill, and snowing.

It stings the skin;
It ages the skin and the shell of life.
There are limited guarantees in this life.

One is aging,
depending on whether or not you're lucky
enough to escape it

Which also depends on your perspective.

Crossroads appear in our routes all the time.

Sometimes, they are clearly signposted;
we know the way without hesitation.
It's our autopilot; there's no reluctance, no
memory of actually crossing the way.

Like the sky on a summer's day – but
definitely not in England.

Sometimes, the crossroads are foggy,
as foggy as the steam on a pair of glasses.

It's a haze, it doesn't allow you to see
clearly.

Undistinguished life and undistinguished
paths.

It is confusing, with an inability to focus.
Concentration failure.

No knowledge of the correct path to take.
You focus on the road you're on, each
individual step that you take.

They take longer than required, life in slow
motion.

The only thing you can focus on is that one
step at that one particular time.

Even the step is unstable, uneasy, and
unreliable.

It is far from guaranteed.

Life's like a bundle of matted wool,
it torments the kitten.
The kitten can become deluded,
believing that it is playing.
Believing it is experiencing some sort of epic
enjoyment.

A bundle of matted wool,
all muddled and knotted.
As a tornado torments a community,
it can continue to torment a cat.
A lifetime of torment with the feeling of the
messy aftermath of the tornado's destruction.

This torment can also become deluded,
seen again as enjoyment.
Much like the playfulness of the fresh,
careless kitten.

If only the brain had the capacity to hold all of the enjoyment;
The majority not just being the torment in our lives.

Memories of a lifetime of uncertainty, judgement and criticism.

The biggest in this life being ourselves.

The question arises, 'Is delusion better than truth?'

More accepted?

The norm in our community.

The norm of life.

# Tired

I feel like a slug. In fact, today, I am a slug.
I have no motivation to function
No inspiration to move
Movement is slow and heavy
Movement is energy that I cannot grasp
My batteries are almost flat
The light shows when you press the button on the remote but there is no power to actually carry out the button's function.
There is no power to carry out required functions.
Instead, I compare myself to a slug.
The eyes on slugs are so close to the concrete, it must pain them.
My eyes feel this pain today.
They itch like an allergy, red and swollen, and they sting like there is too much water being forced into them.
My pupils so miniscule to avoid the light, they are almost invisible.
This makes me as attractive as a slug.
My eyes wish for me to close them.
My body aches. My internal organs are screaming out at me to sleep
Clogged up with fatigue, much like the churning of an IBS patient's abdomen
The sickness a slug must feel on a dry day when a human sees its trail on a wet day
I feel the sickness today.
I feel sick from the bottom of my stomach,
It's been awake that long that it either feels overused or starved.
My existence is starved of sleep.
How I wish I could only count sheep.

# Trust

Betrayal is a personal attack
An attack brought on by your own being
An attack on trust

Trust is a challenging concept

The concept is hardworking, yet extremely high
maintenance
Maintenance is analytical and tiring
It allows emotions to join into the equation

Anxieties, upsets, disapprovals, normalities,
anger and expectations
it's a mixture of ingredients,
it's the need for a full equation, which
includes an answer

It's not a singular being.

Trust is a challenging concept

It is built slowly, precisely,
Brick by brick,
Careful attention being paid to the cement
that gels the foundations.

Trust is a challenging concept

If trust as a concept is challenged, it
becomes vulnerable
You as a being become vulnerable
The vulnerability is a challenge in itself

An attack brought on by your own being

Trust is a challenging concept

The sinking ship does so slowly
The water heavily adding pressure to
the hull
The ship as a being becomes its own brig
A prisoner of the water that surrounds it,
that attacks the cement that gels it together
It erodes the cement slowly, pieces slowly
peeling away, much like the skin after being
sunburnt

Trust is a challenging concept

It can be burnt, like a distinguished flame
Maintenance goes from being tiring to
exhausting. Working hard becomes a mind-
numbing and tedious concept
It remains analytical
It allows the emotions that accommodate it to
become analysed.
This is also exhausting.

Trust is a challenging concept, as is emotion

The anxieties, upsets, disapprovals,
normalities, anger and expectations.
Should I have anxiety about trust?
Should I disapprove of another's actions?
Should it upset me so much that it hurts like
a touched bruise?

Is it normal not to trust another or is it
normal to trust others?
Should others make me angry at myself for
becoming vulnerable because of trust?

Should I be angry that I feel betrayed?
It was my trust that I placed on another,
therefore my expectation;

My unrealistic, as tall as a skyscraper
expectation

Trust is a challenging concept, as is emotion

As is expectation.
Individual to a being and to others

Expectations so high that no one could
possibly reach
If I could alter these expectations, I could
have control,
manage the challenging accompanying emotions,
manage the trust.
Then, vulnerability would not need
maintaining

Neither would trust.

Trust is a challenging concept

Can one person betray another?
Do they own the responsibility?
Or is it because of the high expectations?

Therefore, is it is only betrayal of one's
self and one's being?

My own betrayal.
My own attack.

**Jellybean**

Love is…

Uncontrollable, unpredictable, unimaginable
and unexplainable

It's not being able to imagine a dirt-
flavoured jellybean until you try one

It's that you're aware of its taste and its
reality and accuracy, but at the same time,

have an uneasy feeling of not knowing how
you're aware of it.

How do you know the taste of dirt if never
eaten?

It's the terrifying uneasiness of not knowing
how to escape it if you're not secretly or
openly enjoying it.

It's the petrifying panic the taste buds have
when attempting to work out the taste.

Work out the familiarity.
Even more unsettling, perhaps, is the
unfamiliarity.
It's uncontrollable laughter when you're not
sure of the cause.

Only sure of one thing.
Pant liner required.

It's knowing one type of love your whole life,
then when eating that one jellybean, you
realise it opens up a whole new type of taste
that you never imagined existed.

One taste that's like a tsunami. Powerful, dramatic and relentless.

Washing out all of the security of your understanding of flavours so far with one huge wave of attack

The unpredictability of the flavour of the next jellybean.

Never being able to predict the next flavour and what it means.

It's never knowing how long the taste will last;
Whether a bitter aftertaste will remain and haunt your ability to taste new things.

To love new things.

It's a dream and a nightmare all rumbling and rolling into one.

It's never fair or balanced.

Like the clashing of hot and cold air colliding and creating thunder.
Loud and dominant for all to hear.

The beautiful lightning that is almost certain to be there makes the taste so visible for all who have the ability to see

It spreads like a secondary cancer.

It travels from the heart to the brain.

It clouds judgement, causes internal turmoil
and weakens the ability to function.

It's ruthless and painful and it's hard to
know if the chemotherapy will pay off,
should you try and prevent it; prolong the
agony?
Should you ignore it, live it, feel what's
left to feel; agony and all?
Once cured, it could be beautiful, long-
lasting and energetic, and bring a new lease
of life,
Much like the lightning that accompanies the
thunderstorm.

It's knowing that there must be disagreements
in order for the lightning to come through.

Disagreements between hot and cold to create
the thunder.

It's confusing.

It's always having an empty hole from that one
type of love, which will never be healed once
damaged.

Never being able to be filled with another
type of love.

Like trying to fit a triangle through a
circular hole on a child's shape-sorter toy

It's the intensity and speed of the taste of
the next jellybean.

Once again, not predicted.

It's the jellybean flavour of fresh soap.

Washing away the dirt from the holes that were once empty.

The holes will always remain, yet they are now clean scars, as opposed to the dirty wounds that were once created.

It's having faith that this flavour won't end up haunting you like the last.

It's the consistency of candy floss, wrapping up all past flavours.

All past loves and hates.
All past disagreements.

It's learning to have fun at the fair.

# Knowing myself

I never paid much attention in science
How can I possibly know who I am when I'm not
able to name or locate my internal organs?

How can the organ accurately function without
a name or purpose?

How can I function without knowing my soul?

I haven't got a hole in my heart, but I'm
pretty sure that if I did, it wouldn't affect
my ability to love or to be loved in return

If that is even one of the heart's purposes.

People allow outer appearances to be judged on
numbers, without knowing their inner beings

Where's the logic in that problem?

Is my shell tough like a nut?

Like the crust of the Earth,

the softer layer is seldom shown.

Can a shell be variable?

Sometimes as fragile as an eggshell produced
by a factory hen without enough
grit in its diet.

It's the walking on eggshells around myself,
trying to work out the inner me,

the walking on eggshells around the outer me

Can a nut be judged by a number?
Is a nut judged by its shell?

Some suggest colours represent personality.

Does white mean pure?
If so, I'm certainly not white

Does red mean fury?
If so, there's definitely a hint of red in my
inner self,

and at least once a month in my outer.

It's knowing which colours can be mixed to
make a new one,
Knowing which colours can be seen together,

Knowing which two colours should never be seen
together,

It's figuring out the mixture of colours in my
own palette.

## Heartbreak

Heartbreak is not having a motive.
It stings like a bee and is as deadly as one
Knowing that using the one sting will leave
you dead
But somehow, it still leaves an incredible
pain

Your eyes heavy with the load of water ducts
They can't escape quickly enough
The burning of the throat as you attempt to
hold back the tears
Much like when you swallow a jalapeño, which
you know neither your throat nor gut can
handle.
The music you hear from the impulsivity of the
crying, the nose running and the attempt not
to let it.
The music you like just as much as an East 17
record.
The sound makes you want to hear it less but
somehow it seems louder.

Heartbreak is an emotional ride
You have to wait for the ride to end
It's a rollercoaster you weren't brave enough
to get on in the first place
Why do you never follow your own advice?
Once on the ride, there's no escape

The ride is fantastic, it builds adrenaline,
anxiety, vulnerability and love.
Builds friendship with the person in the seat
next to you,
the best friendship one could have.
It builds trust, understanding and brutal
honesty

You have to grip tight to hold on, both to the
person and the ride.
You feel like you couldn't let go, even if you
wanted to.
Eventually, your knuckles turn white and hands
turn blotchy,
there is no choice anymore.
You have to let go; the ride has stopped.

You never want to go on another rollercoaster

You couldn't beat it, it was the most amazing
ride of your life

Why does the bee have to die?

# Haunting

It is such a daunting word
As scary as the word cancer.
It is a rarity to find anyone comfortable
enough to discuss it

Yet at any one time, everyone has thought
about it

Everyone who has experienced life has a story

They know of a story

As you become experienced in life,
Or maybe even before,
you lose life in yourself, physically and
mentally.
Others lose their souls;
their lives to death

It becomes less of a shock and more of an
acceptance
The closeness almost smothers you
The expectance becomes routine

Death becomes routine
Death is a routine in life

They say there is an afterlife
They say there are ghosts
They say it is just science.

Seeing a ghost does not count as being
haunted.

Is it even a ghost if you actually know the
person? The only difference is that it has
experienced death.

Haunting is as scary as the word cancer
Not everybody is comfortable enough to discuss
it
Everyone who has experience in life has a
story
They know of a story

A story about the afterlife, a story about
ghosts or a story about science

Death can be scary
It is the unknown
Haunting is scary
It is the lack of understanding

It is the unknown

Only perhaps known once dead

Life goes on. Even if you're dead.

# Marriage

Marriage isn't about two people
It's not about two lives

It's the lives that surround the two
Family, friends, colleagues and associates

It's a change, a commitment, a lifetime.

Two people can change,
One person can change.

Family changes.

More are born into it, more die and are
removed from it; marriage creates a wider
family.

Friends change

Some become associates and then friends.
Friends sometimes become associates and
distant memories,

Marriage can create and end friendships.
Most of all, associates change;
You dispose of them frequently and create new
ones frequently.

The commitment between two people can change.

Disposable

The rings that tie the commitment.

Disposable

They can be melted down like a dead body being
burnt in a crematorium.

They can be re-made into another purpose, like
the suggestion of a soul.

What is most important is the constant.

The constant of one person.

Individually.

The morals, the values and the commitment of
one person to another
Whether these are variable or susceptible to
change

Marriage isn't about a party,

an event,

a celebration, or sorrow.

It is a tie.

One person to another

By means of a ring

that's as disposable as a dead body being
burnt in a crematorium.

# World

I do not know much about the world
However, I know this:
We are destroying it.
We destroy it every waking day
Every sleeping night

The wax that feeds the burning candle
Once so bright, it almost radiates warmth like
a slow-burning log fire
It extinguishes as it loses wax, loses energy
We burn the wax,
We burn the energy
The world is being extinguished

Like a house fire extinguished by the enormous
pressure of the fire engine's hose
As each moment passes, a flicker in the candle
appears
It loses it warmth
There is no coal on the fire
Only wood; not even that, chipboard
It blocks up the chimney with the thick,
cloud-like, grey smoke
It's not suitable for the burner, yet we still
choose to burn it
To pollute the chimney
We will maintain it later

There is no ability to maintain something once
damaged
The world cannot be maintained in the future
We have already predicted it
We will continue to contribute to its future

I do not know much about the world
However, I do know this:
There is no better smell than open woodland.

The smell of nature
Not the smell of it burning on the log fire
But the smell of it growing on the acre

I do not know much about the world
However, I do know this:
Individually and collectively, we are
destroying it
We need more of that smell
We need more nature.

**Fairy tale**

A fairy tale is exactly what it says in the
title

A tale

A story

Make believe

A fairy

Not a reality in our world

It is a longing to give hope.
Provides something to look forward to.
An attempt to make things improved.

Expecting things to be superior.
Better than the reality that we live in.
Joyful

Providing a child with an illusion
An illusion of life.

It's cheating.

It provides an expectation.
One that will never be reached.
Disappointment will ooze out of the sequel.

When the child has outgrown the pages,
They realise there is not always a happy ever
after.

Why don't the villains ever win?
After all…

This is the reality that we live in.

## Anger

Anger is a powerful emotion

The term 'emotion' does not do it justice

Quicker and stronger than most

A reaction, responsive

It races through your pulses as if running a
sprint.

Once just dormant, waiting for the starting
gun to fire

Explosive, no longer dormant

It is the magma flowing over the top

Hot with fury, it will destroy anything in its
path

Not a sole traveller,
accompanied by friends

Leading the way for the carrier of upset.

The grey ash left behind once the anger has
retreated

Bitterness at others
Bitterness from one's self pollutes the
surrounding air.

Yet another friend that anger lends a helping
hand to

Let me tell you this…

Anger may be a powerful performing leader

However, it is also a follower

Anger is mostly led by love or hate
Or a kind of personality flaw

Anger and its accompanying emotions are so similar

A line should not be drawn.

Even with the bluntest pencil.

# Illness

A sharp, shooting, no-longer-supressed pain
arises
Stinging and steering the swift way to the
lavatory
Smelling of sewerage

The burning and bubbling of the butt
With a mysterious musical medley, coming from
your gut
A feeling of weakness like the paper covered
in the heavy liquid
Fluids that you would not want to weigh

Feeling as dirty as you have made the toilet
Polluting the rest of your reactions
The calculated churning with an obvious
solution

The solution: the simmering stomach sacrifices
The throbbing throat tortured as it begins
Sick, smelling, once a supressed supper

Uneasy breathing
Spurting, sputtering and spitting out excess
saliva
Weary, watering eyes waver
Retching rapidly as if riding a rodeo

The spiralling temperature
Once natural and neutral, now nauseating
neurotic
Feeling cagey and clammy, then cautious and
cold
Varied, victorious, leaving feelings of
vexation
Lifting light-headedness
Making the room start to sway

Its appears at several parts of the day

The need of protection at the time of the
month
The swollen surroundings, an infection's lunch

The bleeding's a burden
It creates crowded clots that fall from the
cunt
The bleeding is blunt

The drainage of colour from the surface of
your skin
Appearance of panic, looking pale and pimply
This is a feeling of an illness
Illness of the infected.

# Withdrawal

I have an addictive personality
Not the type that makes others addicted
The type that makes me addicted to others
To things:
A new hobby, a new belief, a new craze
An Infatuation
A way of life, a change of life, a new
obsession

Breaking an addiction is exactly as difficult
as it sounds
The placebo effect takes its place
Just the awareness of letting go, alone, can
create a ripple
A ripple large enough to change the direction
of any duck
No matter how fast and hard its feet are
thrusting
Allowing it to be lifted and glide across the
water

The duck needs withdrawal
Bread now weighs it down
How efficient is the duck without its bread
It knows cereal is better for its health, it
hopes.

It hopes the placebo will not last too long

Withdrawal is choosing to have several
addictions
One alone is too much of a risk
Chance is required for luck to take place

Either bad or good, luck is luck

Having the ability to watch an eclipse twice
in a decade.
That is luck.

If, of course, by the time it comes around
again, you have not become preoccupied with
another type of obsession
You can watch it the second time without the
ability to see

It is difficult to watch something without the
ability to see.

It is difficult to know the difference in luck
(bad or good).
It is difficult to know placebo from reality.

**Time**

They say that time is the best healer

This is a lie.

Time is capricious.

Sometimes it flies as fast as a cheetah can run.

Sometimes it is so slow you think it might have stopped.

It still has the same outcome

When you look back, time has still passed

Expectations of healed wounds over time
A lie to their selves

Healed wounds are never truly healed

The slightest memory can re-open them and twist and bend emotions like a meander in a river.

It does not matter how much time has passed in between.

An old, deep wound can hurt as much as a small, fresh, clean wound can sting.

Expectations of others:

They must be better now, they say.
They smiled yesterday and laughed last week

If one thing can be done with time:

1. Take note of the time in between the smile and the laugh!

2. Make an effort to see the hidden tears and tantrums!

3. Don't mistake them for something they're not

4. Take time not to be self-absorbed


Time is a gift we have.

We don't have much given to us in life.

One thing we have in this life is time.

Uncertain of the length we are given.

Unaware of which event in time was most important, when we look back at parts that flew by or hindered.

It was still our time.

The only thing we can do with time is use it. How is for you to decide!

When thinking of time and how much you have, when wondering what time of the day it is, remember one thing.

Time does not heal the wound or cure the illness.

Time is a space that is too occupied.

Use time wisely.

Do not expect time to fix things.

That is our job.

Do not take time for granted.

## Self-harm

I started to think about self-harm,
I thought about harming myself.

The thought kept coming to me,
I wanted to shake it off.

I soon realised that I would not do it.

1. I am not brave enough
2. I did not want others to think I wanted
   attention; that I have a weakness
3. This was the deal breaker:

I hate myself enough already. I do not want to
make myself feel any uglier than I already
feel.

I hope that one day, I will not think about
harming myself.
I hope that one day, it will be history.
Not modern history, but definite in-the-past
history.

A point of no return.

One day, I will realise I need to pick myself
up.

Today is not that day.
I will not need scars as reminders of how I
feel.

The feeling is strong enough for scars on its
own.

I need not wound myself,

I need not rub salt into the wound.

## Doormat

The English language is a complicated beast.
Who came up with all the words?
For example, who named a doormat?

The purpose of a doormat…

To stamp the dirt off your shoes;
To wipe shit on and leave it behind.
To place all your weight on and try to shake
and leave that behind.
To come away feeling clean, refreshed,
acceptable, and then to feel welcomed.

The best thing about doormats…

They are replaceable.
You wear them down.
They age, but only so you as a person do not.

They are reliable and mainly durable.
Some last for years,
depending on the strength of the material.

The foundations that hold it together:

1. It is functional.
2. It is not a friendship.

Replacing the doormat…

The doormat that was once inviting,
an attractive part of the entrance to where
you live your life…
Now dirt-ridden, aged and frayed.
You can dispose of it easily.

Doormats are not accepted,

not in this state.
You do not want anyone to judge you on your
doormat.

After all,
fashions change, people change and their needs
change.

You do not get dirty feet anymore,
you do not need the doormat.

You actually replaced it before you threw it
away.

Just for the record:
  1. Humans are not doormats.
  2. There is only so much shit they can hold
  3. They are named
     'People'
  4. Better yet…
I am a 'person'.

## Circles

My life is like a stuck record,

Not a shining, sparkling, modern CD;

more like the large, dated, plastic LP,

the kind where the scratch does not quite show
up.

However, it is there.

I used to fear I would drown,
I still fear I will drown,
That is one way
I would hate to die.

I know this because…

I am drowning in life.

My life:

I paddle and paddle but there are no available
oars.

The shark has eaten them and I only have the
remains.

A painful splinter.

I gasp but all I can take in is water.

I take that much in, I fear I have water
retention.

I wish I could take in air.

A new burst of exciting energy,
a new burst of life.

The Ferris wheel seems exciting, at first
glance.

My life is like a Ferris wheel.
It's been going around and around in large
circles.

It has a fantastic view at times

At other times, it is daunting.
Bitter cold from the wind as it glides.

Unsteady as the carriages take control,
I am now stuck at the top.

I am also scared of heights.

I am scared to jump.

I am scared to stay.

Instead, I stand perfectly vacant.

I watch others enjoy the ride,

watch their lives make shapes.

Wonderful shapes.

Shapes I do not know how to spell,
shapes I do not even know the names of.

It looks so simple, so easy and so carefree.

How I wish that were me.
I wonder why the only shape I am is a circle.

With an indentation.

It is not even a perfect circle;
I stumble over the indentation simultaneously.

I know it is there.

I see it coming but cannot avoid it;

It is a little exhilarating.

Like when speeding over road bumps,

I bump and bounce until boredom kicks in.

I wonder how long the circle will last.

Let me explain…

When I was younger,

I drew circles with salt (in my head),

this kept the witches away (so I thought).

The circle was never perfect, obviously.

I used to add extra,
just to make sure.

I recently wondered if maybe I am the witch.

Never able to make the perfect shape,

the perfect circle,

the perfect life.

I feel ungrateful,

I feel selfish,

I feel more than one scratch on the record.

I feel anger like the stuck carriage at the
top of the Ferris wheel.

I need oiling.

I feel plenty of indentations,

They cover the shape of me,

I am the circle.

I once heard salt is a slow killer;

As it happens, my circle and I,

well, I am a slug stuck in the circle I made
of salt.

## Dad: The best thing

You were the best thing,
You loved me unconditionally.

I hope you still do

I loved you unconditionally,
although you may not have known.

I still do.

You were a problem-solving and practical
person,
I wish I could solve my problems;
I am trying to be practical

However, I am not you.

I will never be a best thing,
the shadow is too dark;
I struggle to shed any light on it.

My tiny light on your deep, dark shadow is no
match,
I guess my flaws are heavy.

You were the best thing,
You kept your distance.

However, you were always there,
You were in my corner.

I will never be a best thing,
I now have a habit of keeping distance,

I try hard to be there

However, I am not you.

You were the best thing,
You were direct, yet diplomatic,

I will never be a best thing,
I am direct but I cannot master diplomacy.

You were the best thing

Now it is the worst thing

When you have the best, I guess,
when it is gone, it should be the worst thing.

I think I am a worst thing.

I am vacant, feel like time has stopped. The
worst thing is not that I am not you,
You are not you.

# Reality

Sometimes I have a blurred focus,
Dreams and reality merge into one

Questions arise to allow the cloudiness to
clear.

Reality becomes a dream and the dream a
reality,
We live the dream
We create the dream
We live in a reality of both the conscious and
unconscious.

We must trust in our reality.

We should follow our dreams,
they say.
What about the nightmares?
They too are our reality.

We live our nightmares,
we create the nightmares.

I create the nightmares.
Nightmares are also my reality.

The difficulty with blurred focus being, it is
sometimes challenging to be aware of the
boundary:
1. between dreams and nightmares.
2. between the conscious and the
   unconscious.
3. that separates the reality from the
   illusoriness.

Do we need to experience nightmares to
appreciate the dreams?

Do we need to experience death to appreciate
life?

Do we need to experience a blurred focus in
order to appreciate reality?

The reality being that not every question has
an answer.

I do not know the answers,

That is my reality.

**Madgalene**

Grief is a glass vase.

Shattered into thousands of pieces,
the pieces too miniscule to repair.

The edges are sharp and jagged,
they get under the skin.
Wound the flesh.

They leave a pain behind,
way after the wounds are visible.

The pain is comforting,
for it represents love.

The pain is a reminder of the love we shared.

# Idolised couple

*I'd seen it in films*
You know

That fictional love
So powerful that nothing comes close
Where a couple grows old together

Where the couple is not a pair but they are
one

If they were forced to be a pair, they'd still
rely on 'the one'

*I'd seen it in films*
You know

That fictional love that's really a fantasy,
Where opposites attract
Where the pair become one

*I've seen it in reality*
The fantasy became factual

So strong and powerful it cannot be fictional

They grew old together
They had things in common but were still
somehow opposites

*On 28/10/19 cancer took him*
The unit of one was forced to be a pair

Old age had touched their love
But it remained powerful and strong

Although forced to be a pair
She still relied on the one

*On 28/11/19 dementia took her*
They are now once again one.

R.I.P

P.S.: True love exists

## Uno

One thing I have learnt about death is

That love continues.

Dying does not have to mean we have lost;
Grief does not also have to be sadness.

Memories can last a lifetime,

love lasts forever.

It is passed on to us from our loved ones.

As we say goodbye,

we remember to be thankful.

For we hold memories.

We have loved.

Been loved.

And we will continue to love.

## The future

I look forward and not back
I smile and do not cry

(Most of the time)

I see light and not dark
I know dark times lay ahead
They have to because that is life

But I have come through the other side
A better 'me'

I am proud of 'me'.
Be proud of 'you'.
I know you can do it

You can meet me on the other side.
It's not greener but it's lighter.

You CAN learn to smile.
(And mean it.)

Printed in Great Britain
by Amazon